# AN ISLAND ALPHABET
## JAMESTOWN, RHODE ISLAND

BY SHARON McDERMOTT BABBITT     ILLUSTRATED BY DONALD MONG

**An Island Alphabet: Jamestown, Rhode Island**

Copyright © 2022 Sharon McDermott Babbitt
Produced and printed by Stillwater River Publications.

Visit our website at
**www.StillwaterPress.com**
for more information.

First Stillwater River Publications Edition.

ISBN: 978-1-958217-18-4

1 2 3 4 5 6 7 8 9 10
Written by Sharon McDermott Babbitt.
Illustrations by Donald Mong.
Cover & interior book design by Elisha Gillette.
Published by Stillwater River Publications,
Pawtucket, RI, USA.

Names: Babbitt, Sharon McDermott, author. | Mong, Donald, illustrator.
Title: An island alphabet : Jamestown, Rhode Island / by Sharon McDermott
    Babbitt ; illustrated by Donald Mong.
Description: First Stillwater River Publications edition. | Pawtucket, RI, USA:
    Stillwater River Publications, [2022] | Summary: A beautifully illustrated
    alphabet book that celebrates the island of Jamestown, Rhode Island. The
    book features local historic sites, well-known geographic features, and
    local trivia.--Publisher.
Identifiers: ISBN: 978-1-958217-18-4
Subjects: LCSH: Jamestown (R.I.)--Description and travel--Juvenile literature. |
    Islands--Rhode Island--Jamestown--Juvenile literature. | English language-
    -Alphabet--Juvenile literature. | CYAC: Jamestown (R.I.)--Description and
    travel. | Islands--Rhode Island--Jamestown. | English language--Alphabet. |
    LCGFT: Alphabet books.
Classification: LCC: F89.J3 B33 2022 | DDC: 974.56--dc23

FOR NINA—
You are the blue sky of summer,
the laughter in the waves,
the warmth of the sand,
the peace of the day.

# ATLANTIC OCEAN

Jamestown is bordered by the Atlantic Ocean and Narragansett Bay which creates a vital marine ecosystem. Recreational opportunities abound and the waterways also support a busy international shipping channel. The Ocean State boasts a proud maritime heritage that includes hosting the prestigious America's Cup yacht race.

# BEAVERTAIL STATE PARK

Beavertail State Park's 153-acre location at the mouth of Narragansett Bay provides stunning views of the rocky Atlantic coast. Beavertail Lighthouse (1856) has an active, automated beacon that serves as a navigation aid. An aquarium and lighthouse museum are open to the public during the summer.

# CLINGSTONE

"The House on the Rocks" was built on
an outcropping in the East Passage of
Narragansett Bay known as "The Dumplings"
in 1902. Located a quarter mile east of
Jamestown, this privately owned, three-story
shingled summer cottage is an intriguing local
landmark due to its isolated setting.

# DUTCH ISLAND LIGHTHOUSE

Dutch Island lies just to the west of Conanicut Island and is part of Jamestown. The 81-acre uninhabited island is a former military installation now owned by the Rhode Island Department of Environmental Management. There is no public access. The Dutch Island Lighthouse (1857) features a 42-foot tower with an active automated beacon.

## East Ferry

Jamestown's first steam ferry began operating out of East Ferry in 1873 transporting passengers and cargo to and from Newport. It ceased operation in 1969 when the Newport Bridge opened. Today, a small ferry service carries passengers between Jamestown and Newport during the summer months.

# Farms

Watson Farm (1796) is a 265-acre working farm that raises sheep and cattle. It is open for tours in the summer. Several family-owned farms operate on the island, and the famous Belted Galloway breed of cattle is raised here. Jamestown Community Farm encompasses 17 acres and supplies produce to local food banks.

# Golf

Jamestown Golf Course (1901) is a public 9-hole course owned by the town that offers scenic bridge and water views. It is among the earliest golf courses built in New England. A new two-story clubhouse was constructed here in 2021.

# History

The Jamestown Windmill (1787) was once a grist mill that ground corn into cornmeal and animal feed. The domed top (bonnet) of the three-story structure can spin to catch the wind, and the windmill's wooden arms (sails) are covered with cloth to capture the wind and power the mill. The windmill is open to the public in the summer.

# Island Land Trust

The Conanicut Island Land Trust manages the 26-acre Godena Farm that features the largest native pollinator garden in the state. Native plants and trees create a healthy ecosystem and provide food and nesting sites for pollinators. There is an apiary on-site. Parker Farm Conservation Area offers 48 acres of hiking trails. Both properties are open to the public.

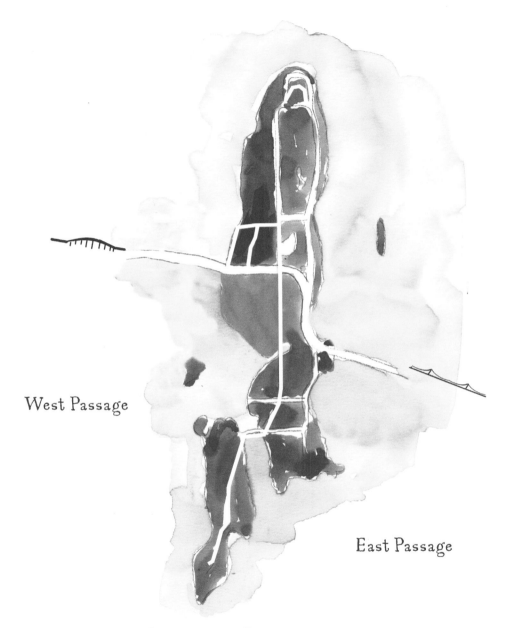

West Passage

East Passage

Conanicut Island

# Jamestown

Jamestown covers Conanicut Island and also includes Dutch Island to the west and Gould Island to the east, both of which are uninhabited former military installations and are closed to the public. Jamestown was incorporated in 1678. It is nine miles long, one mile wide, and is part of Newport County.

# Kayak

Jamestown offers kayakers a variety of options
from exploring sheltered coves to braving
the open ocean in a sea kayak. Some popular
places to launch kayaks include Fort Getty,
East Ferry Town Beach, Potter Cove,
Head's Beach and Mackerel Cove Beach.

# LIBRARY

The Jamestown Philomenian Library (1874) operated out of several locations before moving to its current home on North Road in 1971. This public library is part of the Ocean State Libraries network and offers collections, programs, and services for people of all ages.

# Memorial Square

East Ferry Memorial Square is a small waterfront park area where remembrance ceremonies, special events, and summer concerts are held. The focal point is a 12-foot-high granite monument honoring Jamestown's veterans.

# Narragansett Bay

Narragansett Bay covers 150 square miles and opens to Block Island Sound and the Atlantic Ocean. The bay supports hundreds of varieties of plant and animal marine life along with numerous bird species. Conservation measures are important to protect water quality in this busy bay and estuary.

# Osprey

Jamestown hosts a dozen or so nesting pairs of ospreys each spring and summer. These migrant "fish hawks" spend the winter in South America. Look for their large nests made of sticks on platforms atop poles around the island. Males dive feet first into the water to catch fish to bring back to the nest.

# Playground

The Jamestown Community Playground, built in honor of Officer Ryan J. Bourque, opened in 2018 with all new nautical-themed equipment that replaces old equipment installed in 1990. The playground is located next to the Jamestown Philomenian Library and is a popular hub for families.

# Quality of Life

Jamestown's natural beauty and simple pleasures provide an exceptional quality of life for residents and visitors. The town-owned 41-acre Fort Getty Park and Campground is open seasonally for RV and tent camping. The park offers a public boat launch, beach area, pavilion, and hiking trails.

# Reservoir

The 28-acre North Pond Reservoir is the primary source of public drinking water for Conanicut Island. The area is part of a greenway of protected land that spans the central part of the island. A paved, scenic bike path runs from the reservoir to the Jamestown Community Farm on Eldred Avenue.

# Sanctuary

The Conanicut Island Sanctuary is a town owned parcel located near the on-ramp to the Newport Bridge. The sanctuary provides a safe habitat for wildlife. Birdwatchers and hikers can explore woodland trails that lead to small observation decks with views of Marsh Meadows Wildlife Preserve.

# Town Beach

Mackerel Cove Beach is a municipal beach located on a narrow strip of land between Mackerel Cove and Sheffield Cove on Beavertail Road. The sandy beach and gentle waves create the perfect place to spend a summer day. Swimming, bodyboarding, surfing, and paddleboarding are popular pastimes.

# UNDERWATER

Scuba diving enthusiasts flock to
Fort Wetherill State Park for saltwater dives
that appeal to various skill levels. The calm
waters and sheltered coves are popular with
dive shops for training.

Visibility is usually good, and fish, mollusks,
crustaceans, northern star coral, and eelgrass
are common sights.

# Valmont "Bucky" Caswell Fire Museum

This fire museum features antique firefighting equipment, memorabilia, and photographs from days gone by. A highlight is the restored 1947 Dodge firetruck on display in front of the museum which is decorated for all major holidays. Santa Claus rides in the back during his annual trip around the island.

# Fort Wetherill State Park

Fort Wetherill State Park is a former coastal defense fortification protecting Narragansett Bay that closed after World War II. However, many concrete structures still remain.

The 61.5-acre park offers sightseeing from 100-foot cliffs, hiking, picnicking, fishing, swimming, scuba diving, and snorkeling.

## DEER XING

White-tailed deer are plentiful in Jamestown and have lived here for centuries. They are plant eaters with a reddish tan coat in summer and a grayish brown coat in winter. Some other mammals that live on the island include foxes, coyotes, rabbits, squirrels, and harbor seals in winter.

# YACHT CLUBS

Conanicut Yacht Club (1892) moved to its present location on Bay View Drive in 1954. The Jamestown Yacht Club (1977) uses Conanicut Marina as a home base. Both clubs offer junior sailing programs and adult racing. The annual Fool's Rules Regatta is sponsored by the Jamestown Yacht Club.

# Zeek's Creek

Great Creek, sometimes referred to as "Zeek's Creek," is the main tidal creek in the salt marsh area on North Road at the center of the island. Marsh Meadows Wildlife Preserve supports many species of resident and migrating shore birds, waterfowl, and songbirds, some of which breed here.

CPSIA information can be obtained
at www.ICGtesting.com
Printed in the USA
BVHW091237060722
641405BV00001B/3